# THIS JOURNAL BELONGS TO

_____

_____

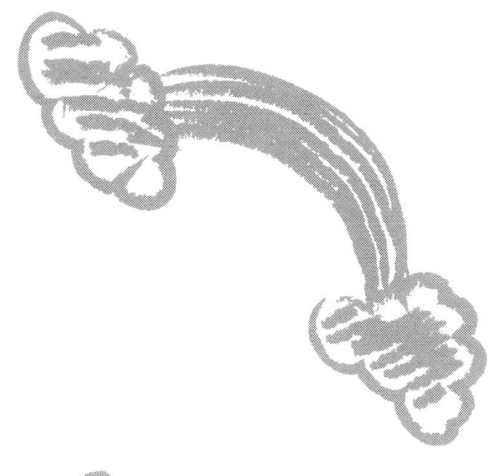

IF YOU ENJOYED THIS JOURNAL,
PLEASE DON'T FORGET TO
LEAVE A REVIEW ON AMAZON.
JUST A SIMPLE REVIEW WILL
HELP US OUT A LOT, THANK YOU!

# In the fall, I See...

[drawing box]

[writing lines]

# The best thing about today...

# List a thing that make you happy.

# I wish I knew more about...

# When I grow up. I want to...

_____

- - - - - - - - - - - - - - - - - - - - - - - - - - - - - - - - - -

_____

_____

- - - - - - - - - - - - - - - - - - - - - - - - - - - - - - - - - -

_____

_____

- - - - - - - - - - - - - - - - - - - - - - - - - - - - - - - - - -

_____

_____

- - - - - - - - - - - - - - - - - - - - - - - - - - - - - - - - - -

_____

# If animals could talk. I would ask them...

<br>
<br>
<br>
<br>
<br>

The best vacation in the whole world would be...

# What I know about rocks is ...

# I made someone laugh when...

_____

- - - - - - - - - - - - - - - - - - - - - - - -

_____

- - - - - - - - - - - - - - - - - - - - - - - -

_____

- - - - - - - - - - - - - - - - - - - - - - - -

_____

- - - - - - - - - - - - - - - - - - - - - - - -

_____

- - - - - - - - - - - - - - - - - - - - - - - -

_____

# No one knows that I...

# If I made dinner, it would be...

_____

- - - - - - - - - - - - - - - - - - - - - - - -

_____

- - - - - - - - - - - - - - - - - - - - - - - -

_____

- - - - - - - - - - - - - - - - - - - - - - - -

_____

- - - - - - - - - - - - - - - - - - - - - - - -

_____

- - - - - - - - - - - - - - - - - - - - - - - -

_____

# I think a great adventure would be...

# I am proud of myself because...

_____

- - - - - - - - - - - - - - - - - - - - - - - - - -

_____

_____

- - - - - - - - - - - - - - - - - - - - - - - - - -

_____

_____

- - - - - - - - - - - - - - - - - - - - - - - - - -

_____

_____

- - - - - - - - - - - - - - - - - - - - - - - - - -

_____

_____

- - - - - - - - - - - - - - - - - - - - - - - - - -

_____

# A special birthday for me is...

# A special birthday for an adult is...

_____
- - - - - - - - - - - - - - - - - - - - - - -
_____
_____
- - - - - - - - - - - - - - - - - - - - - - -
_____
_____
- - - - - - - - - - - - - - - - - - - - - - -
_____
_____
- - - - - - - - - - - - - - - - - - - - - - -
_____
_____
- - - - - - - - - - - - - - - - - - - - - - -
_____

# I'd like to see...

# What I know about rabbits is that...

# This is how I think plants grow.

# Climbing trees is...

_____
- - - - - - - - - - - - - - - - - - - - - -
_____
_____
- - - - - - - - - - - - - - - - - - - - - -
_____
_____
- - - - - - - - - - - - - - - - - - - - - -
_____
_____
- - - - - - - - - - - - - - - - - - - - - -
_____
_____

# For lunch today I...

# If I were a raindrop I'd...

# Noisy times and quiet times are...

# What is a food you hate? Write about it!

If you could design a school uniform, what types
of clothes would you suggest? What colors would they be?

If you could be any animal, which one would you be and why?

Write about the type of music you like to listen to.

# What are you grateful for today and why?

# Write a letter to your future self in 20 years.

# What is your favorite time of day? Explain why?

# The biggest thing I ever saw...

_____
- - - - - - - - - - - - - - - - - -
_____
_____
- - - - - - - - - - - - - - - - - -
_____
_____
- - - - - - - - - - - - - - - - - -
_____
_____
- - - - - - - - - - - - - - - - - -
_____
_____
- - - - - - - - - - - - - - - - - -
_____

# If toys could talk what would they say?

# Tell about one thing you do really well?

Insects, insects everywhere!!! Describe what you see!

What is your favorite room in your home and why?

# Describe your best day ever?

What would happen if it really did rain cats and dogs?

DATE _____

The perfect place in the whole wide world is...

_____
- - - - - - - - - - - - - - - - - - - - - - -
_____
_____
- - - - - - - - - - - - - - - - - - - - - - -
_____
_____
- - - - - - - - - - - - - - - - - - - - - - -
_____
_____
- - - - - - - - - - - - - - - - - - - - - - -
_____
_____
- - - - - - - - - - - - - - - - - - - - - - -
_____

What can you do to help you feel better when you're feeling blue?

# What was fun at your last birthday?

_____

- - - - - - - - - - - - - - - - - - - - - - - - - - - - - -

_____

_____

- - - - - - - - - - - - - - - - - - - - - - - - - - - - - -

_____

_____

- - - - - - - - - - - - - - - - - - - - - - - - - - - - - -

_____

_____

- - - - - - - - - - - - - - - - - - - - - - - - - - - - - -

_____

# What if you grew a tail?

# What makes a person kind?

# What would you do if no one could see you?

When you feel sad, what do you do to feel better?

What would you do if you were in the middle of the ocean and your boat springs a leak?.

# What job would you never want to do?

_____

- - - - - - - - - - - - - - - - - - - - - - -

_____

_____

- - - - - - - - - - - - - - - - - - - - - - -

_____

_____

- - - - - - - - - - - - - - - - - - - - - - -

_____

_____

- - - - - - - - - - - - - - - - - - - - - - -

_____

Where should our class go on a field trip and why?

_____

- - - - - - - - - - - - - - - - - - - - - - - - - -

_____

_____

- - - - - - - - - - - - - - - - - - - - - - - - - -

_____

_____

- - - - - - - - - - - - - - - - - - - - - - - - - -

_____

_____

- - - - - - - - - - - - - - - - - - - - - - - - - -

_____

_____

- - - - - - - - - - - - - - - - - - - - - - - - - -

_____

DATE _____

DATE _____

DATE _____

DATE _____

Made in the USA
Columbia, SC
27 February 2025

54498165R00057